HARMONY OF MY SOUL

(A Progressive Muslim's Spiritual Journey)

Dr. Tita "Nasiha Ali" Gray

TABLE OF CONTENTS

Where do I begin… in life sometimes the beginning comes towards the end.

INTRODUCTION

O believers! Do not ally yourselves with people God
is displeased with. They already have no hope for the
Hereafter, just like the disbelievers lying in their graves.
Qur'an 60:13

Alhamdulillah

The idea of writing this book came when I was going
through significant change, disappointment, and self-doubt. I
began the book as a journal and then it became a way of healing,
finding myself, and recreating a new me. I realized through the
pain, insecurity, and vulnerability that Allah never left my side. I
felt his presence in every teardrop, every cry for help, and every
moment of silence. I felt him saying, continue to learn, to have
faith, to be obedient and trust me…I got you!

I am glad that I delayed publishing this book in the summer of 2022, because on top of every test I faced between 2020
and 2022, the death of my mother on December 26, 2022,
hit me the hardest. When I got word in November 2022 that
she had been admitted into the hospital, something within me
wilted. The flight to Boston didn't feel the same. This time she
wasn't able to speak to me before my travel, so I sat in silence
feeling incredible trepidation. I landed too late in the evening
to go to the hospital, so my friend who I was staying with took
me out to dinner. I tried to be upbeat, but my heart felt full. All
I could think of was my mom; I never slept that evening. First

thing: the next morning I headed to the hospital. Each footstep in the corridor sounded like my heartbeat. Something felt different.

My mom had been in and out of the hospital over the years for many reasons, but I was not prepared for what I saw when I walked into her room. She was disheveled, lethargic, and unexpectedly did not initially recognize me. I cannot put in words exactly what my core felt, but maybe if I explain our relationship, it might give some idea of the impact.

My mom was my best friend, and I was hers. I was given her middle name, beautiful smile, and love for music. Growing up, she always gave me room to be myself, at times probably too much room, but each mistake made me grow. She was fearless in protecting me and my brother, probably to a fault where he's concerned. I can remember as a young girl how proud my mom was of my academic and sports achievements. She encouraged me to pursue all of my dreams. She never told me I couldn't achieve something; she just reminded me that no one does everything well. She taught me to focus on what I loved, what made me passionate, and I followed her advice to this day.

Mom and I wrote each other love letters, yes, beautiful, and sentimental handwritten letters confessing our undying, unconditional, and forever love of one another. They would bring so much comfort for us. It was our way of being closer to one another. I tried to get her to move in with me, no matter where I lived coast to coast, but she would always graciously decline. So instead, we took amazing trips together whenever she would visit me. One of our favorite trips was Las Vegas. She had so much fun using the slot machines that I just sat on the side watching her and enjoying her joy. There are no words that can express the pain I felt (and still feel) when I realized she would never leave the hospital, and that we would never speak again, that God was calling her home. If I wasn't absolutely sure that my mom was in paradise with Allah, I honestly don't know how I could function, particularly since she was my rock during everything I had been through beginning of 2020.

Twenty-twenty (2020) began with a new job, friends and family drastically affected by COVID, a new relationship, and becoming Muslim. For me, like others, that was a year of transition, struggle, and isolation. I believe that the antiracism movement, a pandemic, and the repulsive, inhumane racist acts spawned by a corrupt president left all of us searching for meaning, trying to understand our life journey, and coming to the aid of one another. I witnessed so much despair, confusion, and loss. During this period, my emotional, physical, and spiritual mindset was being tested repeatedly. My journey during that time began with gratitude because my job wasn't in jeopardy, which meant neither was my home or way of living. Although I wasn't able to visit my mother, I was content that she was safe and healthy.

Although my life was filled with gratitude, I was longing for companionship during this time of isolation and…I found it, lost it and, with time, began to find myself. In addition, I was seeking spiritual growth and Islam opened that door. After what I experienced over two years, I felt compelled to write about my journey because it had been such a spiritual manifestation and awakening. Everything around me was changing and taking on a new meaning. My life drastically changed at a period when most people would prefer to be settled, maybe retired, traveling, etc.

I felt the need to write this book for anyone going through a transformation and needing to find some commonality in the conflicting battles they were feeling and understand how to get through them. The most significant thing that I can say is that once your mind, body, and soul work together with the powers of the universe, you'll be on a path to harnessing your greatest possibilities. Know thyself and your truth will illuminate your highest potential and purpose. Remember, Allah only wants us to be our best selves. When you have situations that look impossible, when you don't see a light at the end of the tunnel, don't talk yourself into disbelieving, believe in praising God *for all conditions* and strengthen your faith.

In this book, I'll highlight how your thoughts, actions, and emotions can manifest and transform the steps of your life journey. Many of us have experienced trauma and damaging messages from those that should have loved and protected us, and we've internalized those voices to the extent that they control our future. It doesn't matter if you're experiencing adversity, understanding that you are exactly where you're supposed to be is the main point. This is only a test and if you stay in faith, you'll be able to handle anything.

I am inviting you to eliminate anything that is holding you in pain, self-loathing, and depression. If you are in conflict over your income, divorce, sexuality/identity, or anything else, need not look to people to justify your relevance, seek God for answers, protection, and comfort, for He is all you need to accept that you are perfect just as you are. Nothing changes over night but when you let go of the cloak that covers your true destiny, you will discover your authentic self, the one that God always wanted you to be. Through faith and patience, I found my truth; it is up to you if this resonates enough for you to find yours. I pass this on as a message from Allah. He guided my words and thoughts.

CHAPTER ONE

Prisoner of War

The Beginning

I am blessed to say that I had a happy childhood. My mom, brother and I lived with my grandmother in a brownstone in what is now an affluent section of Boston. My aunts, uncles, and cousins were always visiting. I can remember big holiday dinners and a lot of laughter. Growing up my favorite cousins were Nancy and Stephanie, and although I was younger, we were still close enough in age to have similar likes. It was fun when I would visit them, or they visited us. Our family unit was very diverse, but it wasn't really considered that back then. For example, one of my cousins was born a woman, but she always identified as a man. No one seemed to trip about it. We just treated her in the manner that her mother did, my mom's twin sister. I don't doubt that she would have been a transgender man if it were an option 50 or more years ago.

There were things I went through that were unfortunately categorically typical for a young black girl. I experienced racism, sexual molestation, and bigotry, yet because of my mom and grandmother, I always knew that I could persevere through anything. I was a very precocious child, some of that was inherent, some based on my mom and granny ingraining it in me that I always had to be better, dress better, talk better, and be smarter because of racism. Speaking of racism, I remember waiting to cross the street on my way to elementary school and being called a little nigger by white men in a car. Although there were adults standing there, no one said a word in my defense. It is strange that bystanders don't realize that they are as bad as the assailants. That moment never left me, it changed me, as does most traumatic events when you're young.

I never shared with my family anything about my first experience being "rubbed on" because I knew it would cause dissension. I didn't even share with my cousin Nancy, who was always like a big sister to me. I was between 6 and 8 years old, too young to know when it was initially happening that it was wrong, but years later, like most situations that were traumatic, reflection brought on reality. I thought to myself that it wasn't worth causing issues over, especially for my mom, and I felt like it didn't leave a scar. In hindsight, it damaged me. I became sexually active at a young age because of those things that were done to me. There are many amazing books that discuss the carnage that is left when children are molested regardless of the extent of the act. It is something that changes your mind and body. I thank God every day for turning every bad situation into a strength, an experience, instead of baggage, and a truth that I can share to help others.

Granny

Black patent leather shoes, a frilly laced dress, and ribbons around each of my long braids were all I needed to feel like the prettiest little girl dressed up for church on Sunday. I looked forward to those early mornings with my Granny. Waking to her making breakfast, talking about what she was going to make for dinner, and spending just a little time fussing about the family she cleaned for, yet expressing her gratitude for a job. I always felt special walking to church with her. It was as if I was the smartest and cutest child on earth. She always walked very straight, with her head held high, gleaming with pride. Being a domestic worker never phased her, never made her feel lesser. She was too blessed. Although she walked with pride, I know that cleaning for someone was not the life that she wanted for me based on how often she would repeat *"you must get your education, no one can ever take that from you."* Whenever I completed another degree, I believe she was in heaven saying, *"you did good."* When someone influences you positively, it never goes away. It remains like a voice of reason, a guiding principle that plays repeatedly in your mind, especially during moments of turmoil. How often have you felt something in your gut telling you to *"move forward"*? How often do you listen? Manifestation is key.

My Granny was born in 1895 and migrated to American from Jamaica in 1920. She came through Canada to avoid Jim Crow laws. She belonged to an Episcopalian church and had been a member most of her life in America. The African American and Caribbean affiliation with the Episcopal church goes back to the nineteenth century. Absalom Jones was the first black priest ordained in the Episcopal Church in 1804. Granny loved church, loved God, and loved me. Although I don't recall most of my time in church, I remember spending time with her learning the 23rd Psalm, 10 commandments, and other scriptural verses that she deemed important. To her, these biblical doctrines were a part of everyday values, a way of living, supporting humanity, and showing gratitude to the Almighty. She taught me how and encouraged me to say my prayers before going to bed, or going to sleep, when I ate, and when good or bad things happened. Her love for God always comforted me, made me feel safe, and instilled the ideals that I carry with me today. There's not a day that goes by that I don't miss her, wish that I could lay my head on her lap, or hear her voice again. My soul continuously calls out for her essence, spirit, and calm. My prayer is that everyone has someone from the past, in the present, or in the future that brings them the joy that I had with my grandmother.

Reality

My relationship with God became real around the age of seven. It was a warm day in Boston. Fall was beginning and so was my third-grade school year. My mother was taking me shopping for new shoes and clothes. I held her hand as we entered the department store. I believe it was called Jordan Marsh. This school year was different. I didn't have to wear secondhand clothes from Goodwill, and I was crazy excited. We were having a great day until the elevator to the third-floor shoe department opened, and within moments of walking in, Mom immediately froze. I was oblivious until she grabbed my hand and said, *"we have to leave!"*. I immediately looked at her in disbelief and then turned toward her gaze. Unbeknownst to me, my father was sitting there with his wife and baby. That image of the man who was my father, with his family, never left me. I didn't understand why he hadn't taken me shopping, why my mother was so upset, and *why* I wasn't getting my new shoes. I didn't understand why I didn't have my father.

Upon returning home, I turned to Granny for consolation. As I put my head in her lap, I asked in my sad and confused eight-year-old voice, why my father didn't love me and buy *me* shoes? The tears flowed, filled with confusion and heartache. I could sense Granny's anguish as she explained that the man I saw today only helped my mother make me, but he's not my only father. God is also my father. I remember the perplexed look that I gave her. I told her I never saw or talked to God, so how could he be my father? She asked me if I ever got visits from, talked to, or received gifts from the man my mother said was my father, I said no. She told me that for the rest of my life God will protect and love me, answer my prayers if I'm a good girl, and when I'm sad I should go to Him for answers. She said, he's your only father now! From that day forward, I believed God was my *only* father. Of course, my elementary and middle school friends looked at me like I had two heads when they asked where my father was, and I would say, *"God is my father."* To this day, when I explain that I have never known another father other than God, it is perceived that I am being religious when it is my reality, not even close to being religious in intent. The only father that I have turned to for love, guidance, protection, and forgiveness has been God. I truly know no one else.

My Grandmother used to implore me to always go to college, get a good job, and keep God first. She was my foundation and refuge, my voice of reason, and my first understanding of God and God-like qualities. It was her influence during the most important times of my childhood that molded me into the woman I have become. Her many lessons taught me about humility, fear, judgement, and shame. I was able to show my gratitude to her when I was asked to create a TED Talk. I made it a dedication to her impact on my life. My Grandma's teachings were the catalyst for my relationship with God and probably my journey to Islam. Although my Granny influenced my life significantly, my mom was my inspiration.

Mommy

My mom fought many demons while my brother and I were young, but she loved and protected us the best way she knew how. She worked full time while Granny took care of us. What I loved most about my mother was her love for music and sports, both of which played a big part of my life. We listened to her favorite singer, the great Sarah Vaughan, while Mom would sing along from the depths of her soul. She shared with me she had always wanted to be a singer, but her fears and lack of encouragement stalled her pursuit of the one passion she loved most. I loved my Mom very much and wanted to do anything to make her proud, but as a teenager, I had many struggles and moments of immense confusion.

My mother, for years, dealt with her issues by being a functioning alcoholic. I loved her, but I hated her drinking and often replaced the alcohol with water, hoping that she would change. She told me years later as an adult that she knew I was replacing her liquor and that it used to make her feel bad knowing that I didn't like it. She did eventually kick the habit, but it came when I was already finding my source of comfort in a boyfriend, at fourteen years old. Even though I wasn't promiscuous,

I shouldn't have been having sex or drinking at such a formative age. That was a time in my life filled with dreams of being a teacher, traveling the world, and having a family, yet at the same time encumbered with conflict over my identity and the need for guidance. Feeling that I had no one to turn to had become a common theme during that time in my life and unfortunately, it is still embedded somewhere deep inside my soul and spirit.

My boyfriend was everything to me during my teens (and we're still friends). We shared many commonalities, including music, learning, and sex, but I had an intense attraction to women. For some reason, it didn't seem strange. It made me feel at peace. It was like the essence of a woman made my heart race, eyes shine, and spirit sing. My imagination would soar with wonder and glee at the thought of embracing a woman. I just didn't know what to do with it nor who I could speak to about it, so I just kept moving along in my naivety and curiosity. According to healthychildren.org, feelings of being "different" appear throughout childhood, although it may not be clear to the child what the feelings mean. Children may explore gender and relationships before kindergarten, so "coming out" and communicating these feelings of being different with others may happen. For many kids, gender and sexual identity becomes apparent around adolescence as they develop certain characteristics and stronger romantic attractions. This was definitely the case for me.

Early Loss

Around the age of sixteen, I became filled with anxiety when my cycle didn't come for two months straight. I was terrified, and again, didn't know who to speak to about it…and then something happened. One evening, I began having severe abdominal pains. I strolled towards the bathroom, bracing myself with my hand along the wall. I looked down to see that I was covered in blood. I could barely walk but made it to the bathroom with the thought that my cycle showed up…late and with a vengeance. I stood in shock, not knowing what to do at the sight of the plethora of blood I was losing. Becoming light-headed, I sat on the toilet, doubled over in excruciating pain, and suddenly, felt a mass pass through my body so large that the water in the tank splashed. I was having a miscarriage. After about 30 minutes of sitting in pure bewilderment, I stood up, glanced at the toilet, which was filled with blood and large clots, flushed the toilet, and laid on the floor crying for what seemed like eternity. There was so much blood that I had to use a towel for triage. After about an hour, I could stand long enough to clean myself up and figure out, between me and God, what to do next. Telling my mother that I had bad cramps, I laid in bed for two days, sick, in pain, and feeling alone. I told no one, including my boyfriend. That experience was a moment in time that changed something in my spirit. It created a hole that took years to fill because I kept that trauma a secret.

After my boyfriend served in the Navy, I started hanging out with a diverse, eclectic group of people and my experiences with women began. I met a woman about twelve years my senior and a fire was awakened in my soul that never died. She taught me how to feel with my mind and be aligned with my spirit and truth in ways that I never imagined possible. It was a strange time because I didn't tell my friends what I was experiencing. However, they noticed I was preoccupied with something or someone and it was changing the person who they knew me to be. I began having experiences that changed me from a girl into a woman, but my maturity and resolve were tested again.

Unfortunately, at only 22 years old, had a benign tumor on my ovary, and it was determined that I needed a partial hysterectomy. There was a part of me that just surrendered with the likelihood that I was not going to be able to have children naturally. I tried to make peace with the feeling of loss, the grieving, even yearning for what would never be for me. The longing for that hole to be filled, fulfilled, and healed presented itself in my dreams, meditations, and relationships. The trauma from a miscarriage and then a hysterectomy at such a young age made me feel inept and lacking. In the book *The Body Keeps Score: Brain, Mind and Body in the Healing of Trauma*, the author states *trauma is a fact of life, and one in five Americans has been molested; one in four grew up with alcoholics; and one in three couples have engaged in physical violence.* That book, among others, helped me to face my own deeply rooted trauma. Trauma can be so profoundly embedded in our being and it's not until we sometimes suffer trauma again that we realize there is a critical problem that needs to be addressed. Have you experienced loss when you were young? Do you ever wonder how you cope with that being taken away? Do you tell yourself *"I don't care any longer?"* or *"I just stopped thinking about it?"* If so, I invite you to pause and see if you are displaying behavior to fill that void. I began writing this book after facing trauma again from a toxic relationship and realized that my desperate need for a family was based on the distress of having a miscarriage. How do I know? I put my all into that relationship and everyone who loved me could see it was toxic, but because it filled my hopes and dreams of a family, I ignored the warnings and trauma slapped me again. Only faith and patience prevailed, through Allah's mercy. Even though we are not regularly aware, Allah is always blessing us with His miracles and answering our prayers.

Awareness

In the book *Secrets of Divine Love*, the author, a. Helwa, states, *"an unnamed mystic said, God sees the black ant on a black stone in the darkest night, so how could he not see the pain of a faithful seeker?"* Moreover, through adversity than good times, I have tried to make sense of my life, purpose, identity …and in a lot of ways, spirituality. Spirituality was something that in the past, I kept to myself during times of struggle. I have always known that God was covering me, but since I didn't know the correlation between patience and faith, my way of escaping was by throwing myself into learning, pursuing a higher education, and establishing a career. Most people looked at me as being strong and resilient, but I was trying to find balance, meaning, and a way of focusing inward. I knew I needed a deeper connection to God, and in the year 2020, I found that in Islam.

I was always interested in and wanted to explore a better sense of Islam. As an openly gay woman, I didn't believe that Islam would embrace me, even though Allah had always loved and blessed me. I felt that to be Muslim, I would have to change my identity, the essence of what He created me to be, and it didn't feel authentic. For one, I do not wear dresses, I do not cover my hair in public unless I choose to, and I drink alcohol socially at times. These were always things that made me feel unwelcome. I could not see myself being welcomed in a Masjid because of how I looked; where did I fit in? Although God has always been a major part of my life, and I gave thanks for every blessing or hardship, I did not see myself being welcomed by other Muslims because I was not traditional. In the book Homosexuality in Islam, the author Scott Siraj al-Haqq Kugle states, *"Though some gay, lesbian, and transgender Muslims may abandon their faith, many others refuse to relinquish their identity as Muslims. They retain their religious belief in the revelation of the Qur'an and their personal practice of Islamic rituals, even as they are persecuted or ostracized in their religious communities."* I find it disturbing that people must feel fear, isolation, and despair to practice something so private as their relationship with God. Are there any human beings that are the same? Absolutely not. We all have different DNA, cultures, experiences, beliefs, trauma, interpretations, dreams, preferences, aspirations, consciousness, feelings, abilities, intelligence, creativity, wants, and needs. Don't you agree? If you agree, and you believe we are all made by Allah, then why do so many people want us to act the same, think the same, dress the same, interpret the same, and have the same relationship with Allah? I assume that the explanation is that they do everything perfectly. None of us are better than the other and thus we should not ignore the differences that Allah created in all of humankind. I am blessed to be different. My unique thinking and perspectives have helped hundreds of people in some manner of their personal and professional lives, whatever that might look like to them.

I became a Muslim because I fell in love with the story of Muhammad (pbuh). I fell in awe of how he respected and treated the women in his life. I felt amazed at his empathy and kindness shown to prisoners of war. I felt gratitude for his ability to forgive and be patient with people that ridiculed and abused him. In 2020, I celebrated Ramadan not as a Muslim but as a way to honor God, and as a result, Allah showed me Islam. Allah showed me how to pray, and he let me see my imperfections were beautiful. Allah tested my faith by taking away everything that I adored, loved, and aspired to have for two years straight. I am not exaggerating in the least. Everything. I found myself behaving and reacting to situations in uncharacteristic ways, so much so that many people who knew me well were perplexed. I realized that when Allah decided to give shaytan (devil) the reigns to test the faith of his believers, anything may happen. As for me, I found myself doing all kinds of foolishness, agreeing to things I normally never would, and trusting people that told me and showed me "in writing" how they would treat me badly. Hence, the work of the devil and his minions is real, but when you're strong in faith and patient with Allah's lessons, the rewards are greater than you can imagine.

In the year 2020, one person whom I love deeply changed the course of my religious path with no knowledge or intention that he was doing it. My friend Aatif, who I call my big brother, helped me to really understand Islam. Alhamdulillah. Our love for each other, our family, and, most importantly, Allah, made us inseparable. It wasn't just our conversations that made me love this man, it was my observation of his character. He was hardworking, honest, caring, a great father, and peaceful. I always admired his knowledge of Allah. He would reference Him with everyday occurrences, but it never sounded like he was preaching or making a religious statement, it was just a matter of fact. I realized rather quickly that I could talk to him about anything and wouldn't be judged. He was the catalyst that made me feel comfortable and confident in Islam. Actually, during my whole transition through 2020 and 2022, I believe he kept me alive or at least sane - and I am not exaggerating.

Often in life, the most meaningful gifts that we receive do not come wrapped with a bow, a warm smile, and a celebration. Instead, they come with hardship, disappointment, and when we are facing our darkest moments. It's always darkest before dawn. We tend to forget or overlook that a new day begins at 12am. Allah began the day when it was dark for a reason. He wanted us to have faith that although it may be dark, the light of the day will always be upon us. If you believe that when you go to bed at night, there will be sunlight in the morning, you should also believe that when you sit in the darkness of despair, there will eventually be the light of joy. In Christianity, it is said that Jesus addressed a group of people, saying, *"I am the light of the world. No followers of mine shall wander in the dark; he shall have the light of life."* Light gives life to your soul and shows the way through the darkness. You just have to have faith that for every new day is an opportunity for change.

CHAPTER TWO

Manifestation

Manifestation is making everything you want to experience and feel become a reality through your thoughts, emotions, actions, and beliefs. According to Angelina Lombardo, author of The Spiritual Entrepreneur, *"If we are truly desiring a future different from our past, we will have to understand where to begin. And it starts with the present moment."* One of the most important lessons that I have learned and still trying to perfect is the process of letting my conscious mind stay in the present moment and focused on what needs to happen to bring direction, awareness, and discernment while freeing the subconscious mind to manifest my intentions with patience and gratitude. Patience requires us to regain our priorities, our time, and our power to respond to life with a firmly grounded sense of who we are. It is the best gift that we can give ourselves. Patience is waiting in grace and faith, knowing that you have no control of the outcome, only control of the present moment, and having gratitude for the ability to experience the abundance of your patience and the will to attract what you desire. Demonstrating gratitude for the small things is one of the best ways to get out of a pattern of negative thinking. It helps take conscious account of everything you have in your life.

Throughout my life, I have made many mistakes, accomplished many milestones, and always turned to Allah when troubled, happy, sad, and/or confused. Through experience, I have discovered a strong correlation between one's life purpose and how thoughts manifest into truth. In the book *The Secret*, Marci Shimoff states, *"Once you begin to understand and truly master your thoughts and feelings, that's when you see how you create your own reality. That's where your freedom is, that's where all your power is."* I have countless moments when I would say something like, "I'm going to live there" or "I'm going to have that car" or I'm going to work there" and in time…it would happen. I didn't know at the time that what I was manifesting in my thoughts and beliefs would become reality. I always said these things at the moment and the intent felt real. It was probably real because it was the path that God had for me all along.

My First Love…Music

One of the earliest moments that I can remember when my thoughts manifested themselves into truth was when I was seventeen, underaged, and visiting my first dance club. I sat the whole night watching the DJ. I was mesmerized and told myself that I was going to be a DJ. I visualized myself behind those turntables, people dancing to my music, and within one year, I was working at a club. That gig turned into a career in the music industry and a hobby that I still practice forty years later. When I began my first job at indie label Sleeping Bag Records, I dreamingly looked out the window and said, "I am going to be working in a high-rise building overlooking Central Park," and within one year, I was working for Elektra Records in Rockefeller Center on the 23rd floor. When the realization hit me, I just sat there for what seemed liked forever…and I thanked God. What seemed to be a dream, or maybe a coincidence, was actually the path God willed for me.

As with all the good times, there will be disappointment. I worked in the music industry for nine years before the bottom fell out and I found myself jobless. Resume after resume, nothing was transpiring, not even a rejection letter. Day after day, on my knees, I would ask God to help me find employment, yet before I could stand up, my thoughts would turn negative and to doubt that nothing would happen. I recall this pattern going on for a couple of months until one day I angrily cried out to God *"if you are the almighty then you deal with this crap, I can't do it any longer!"* Unbeknownst to me at the time, I was surrendering, letting go and letting God. One week after I surrendered, I received a call about a position. I met with the director and was offered the job. It didn't hit me until months later, but the biggest lesson I learned from that moment was that you can't simultaneously have faith and fear. If you ask God for help, you must stand back and patiently wait in gratitude.

Follow Your Purpose

After the attack on the World Trade Center and a feeling of being complacent, my intuition kept telling me it was time to leave NYC. The feeling penetrated my soul, gnawing at my gut repeatedly. I didn't know where to begin, but on a whim, I contacted an acquaintance from NYC who was thoroughly enjoying her move to Northern California. When I mentioned I was looking to relocate, she told me to pack my bags, and in total faith, I did just that. It was not an easy transition, actually, it came with a lot of anxiety and moments of doubt. California had a completely different culture than the east coast, not for better or worse, just different. I often felt alone. My mind was telling me to go back to New York, but my soul was telling me to stay. I knew I didn't want to go back feeling like a failure or deemed to not handle adversity, so I persevered.

Within a few months, with God's mercy, I landed an executive position at a Fortune 500 company in San Francisco. I was grateful for the opportunity, enjoyed the work, however I had no passion for the industry, and again I found myself missing home and my mom. In an effort to stay the course, I decided to enroll in an MBA program at San Francisco State University. Going back to school was exciting. I gained close friendships and a sense of belonging with my cohort. It was exactly what I needed to fill up those lonely moments, and unbeknownst to me at the time, it was going to open another important door. In the beginning of the Qur'an, Al-Faatiha says *"show us the straight path,"* my journey was on the straight path, but I did not realize how significant the steps of that path were about to impact my future.

Upon completion of my degree, that unsettling feeling resurfaced, and I knew it was time for change, that it was time to follow my purpose. I made the decision to leave my employer and go after my dream of being a college professor. Throughout my life, my most invasive dreams included being a professor and having a life partner. I found myself once again stepping out on faith. I decide to move to San Diego, where I was in a long-distance relationship and subsequently, pursue teaching positions. There are times when Allah moves us towards people, places, or things that are chaotic and full of turmoil. It's hard to understand at the time that it is a test for our betterment. During my relocation to San Diego for a relationship and a career in academics, I did not know that the relationship would turn toxic and leave me suffering from mild PTSD for years to come. Even though we were loving towards each other's family, it was filled with constant verbal and emotional turmoil. Despite the mess, shame, and disappointment, I landed a teaching position at San Diego State University (SDSU) within three months. How it transpired was a miracle…no…it was Allah moving me forward on my destiny, regardless of the adversity I placed myself in.

One afternoon, I happened to be speaking to my friend Markus. We had worked together previously, became very close and looked out for each other all the time. He suggested I attend an event at SDSU in his place as a speaker, since he knew I wanted to get into higher education. He said that the subject was within my expertise, and they would benefit, so I graciously accepted. The event itself was lackluster, however, the other speakers were amazing and dynamic. As it turned out, one of the speakers who was impressed with me was a professor in the College of Business. We began talking, and I told her of my aspiration to teach. She suggested I meet with the department chair and that she would set up the introduction once she was back from vacation. I was so excited and told her I was humbled and would be honored. The event was in May. I got an email in July from Dr. Shore saying that she'd like to meet with me. We met at a Starbucks, and I liked her right away. She explained that while she believed I would be a great fit at the College of Business, I had no prior experience and there was a process to hiring, which began with the current adjunct staff, then the associate professors and professors. Since I came with no expectations, I was grateful for her taking the time to meet with me. I told her I would keep looking for other opportunities and would stay in touch with her throughout my journey. She told me not to expect anything in the near future…but God had other plans.

It was a hot summer day on August 20th. I was sitting on the living room floor doing research and applying for teaching positions when an email appeared, *"Hello. It's Lynn Shore. I was wondering if you'd be interested in teaching a class in Organizational Behavior? If you're interested, please let me know asap because classes begin on August 28th."* I was so ecstatic and filled with joy that I jumped up and almost broke my laptop. I screamed at my partner to please read it again while I jumped up and down like a little girl. I answered back with a resounding yes and by the next morning was offered another class and told that two classes made me eligible for benefits. My relationship ended soon after, but as I stated, God had other plans. Welcome to San Diego State University!

Sometimes Allah puts you in the most painful situations to get you to your higher self. My time spent at SDSU was one of my greatest accomplishments. As a professor and administrator, I received an award for excellence every semester that I taught there. I loved my students and think of many of them as family to this day. To them, I was more than a former teacher or administrator, I was a confidant, and family. I always started off a new class by introducing myself and giving a little background. I would speak about my corporate experiences and, in particular, my time in the music industry because it made me more relatable to them, one student in particular.

I remember the day that Aleksey walked into my class. He came in later than most of the other students and sat way in the back. This became his routine. One day when class ended, he asked if he could meet with me to talk about the music industry. I told him yes, of course, and we went out to lunch. Aleksey was a writer and producer and shared his hopes and dreams about music. I shared my experiences, but more importantly, I listened to him and provided feedback. As we got to know each other, I could see that our relationship had a deeper meaning and purpose, so I made the conversation more personal. I asked him why he seemed lethargic in class, participated little, and just seemed uninterested. He shared that his mother had recently passed away from cancer and he was grieving for her loss. He explained that music was not only his passion but had become his refuge from the pain. He didn't want to be in school, but he promised his mom that he would finish. I realized immediately that I wanted and felt a calling to love and guide this beautiful young man through college and life. Over time, even when he was no longer in my class, we spoke regularly. Our relation became what both of us needed, one of a mother and son. One day, I remember it well, he asked if I would be his Godmother and if he could call me mom. I said a resounding "yes" and my heart filled with joy and satisfaction. It filled the hole of motherhood that I always desired and the hole of loss and grief that he needed. Eight years later, and he now has a son which I call my grandson. Allah is all knowing and with time and patience heals all wounds of the soul.

My time at SDSU included becoming a professor, Assistant Dean and completing a doctorate degree. I followed my purpose regardless of the obstacles because God willed it. I didn't realize that while I was going through adversity, God was molding me into being a great teacher and mother. My gratitude to God and his mercy were demonstrated time and time again. It took an enormous amount of tenacity to manage the rigor and isolation that you encounter when pursuing a terminal degree while working full time. There were countless days when I didn't know if I could continue but my mother always encouraged me to be strong and to know she was proud. I often wished that I had a partner to help me make a meal, draw a bath, lay my head on, cry too, etc. but I persevered. I became aware during those moments, that God was with me, and for every day that I could rise, I was given another chance to get through the day. Alhamdulillah. I not only finished my degree, but I was also the first in my cohort to complete all my requirements. A Doctor of Education was born.

Whenever Allah tests his people, he washes off our sins. He plainly states that Muslims should pursue help through patience and prayer, and He will eventually relieve the hardships. The Qur'an tells us to stay calm during the difficult times and train ourselves to stay patient instead of breaking down and losing temper.[1] A lifelong aspiration to be in academia had come to fruition with patience and gratitude. I fulfilled a lifelong dream once again; however, my life would take a turn.

Change

I was accepted into a Management program at Harvard University with the intention of one day landing a Vice President position at a university. The timing of this program and being back in the Boston area were a Godsend. I got to spend precious time with my aunt, my mom's twin sister, who was dying from cancer. It was filled with memorable moments between me, her, and mom. We laughed, joked, and made fun of each other like only family could do. At times, those visits were surreal. It took every bit of strength that I had to be in class all day, then pick up my mom and head to the hospital to be with my aunt until visiting hours ended. I needed to be there for my mom. Losing a loved one is unquestionably a grief-stricken and disturbing

---

[1]   https://www.theislamicquotes.com/life-lessons-from-quran/

time, especially for family. Although according to the Qur'an 2:156, a soul belongs to Allah and will return to Him in time, it is still painful facing our loved one's passing away. Only those people who have experienced it can truly know the depth of pain it brings when it happens. It hurts so deeply in your core that sometimes you feel numb with emotion. The experience of spending time with someone that you love, knowing that it will be your last time hearing their voice and seeing them, is something that you never forget. As I reflect on those moments, I wish I had been Muslim at the time because I would have found solace in celebrating her journey to Allah. The thoughts of my aunt weighed heavy on my mind, and especially when I was on the plane back to San Diego. Not long after I returned to San Diego, my aunt passed away. In addition, one of my cousins died suddenly. It became painfully apparent that I needed to move back east to be closer to my family. When I told my friends and colleagues about my decision, they were understanding yet saddened that I was leaving. There was a huge part of me that was disheartened too yet the only thing I could think of was sacrificing for my family, especially my mother.

I spent most of my free time preparing and contemplating my next professional move. I began reading books about being a senior officer, I saw myself in that role. I aspired to be a VP at a university, so I prayed on it, and met with friends that were VPs to understand the lay of the land from their perspective. I began the process of looking for employment and interviewed at two institutions, I accepted a job in Miami, Florida, at Miami Dade College. Although it wasn't at a VP level, I felt it would be a great experience working at a Community College since my doctorate degree focused on Community College Educational Leadership. In addition, when I lived in New York, going to Miami during the winter for a weekend wasn't unusual. I learned quickly that visiting some place for a weekend and living there, were two mutually exclusive events. It didn't take long before I realized I had made a terrible and costly decision. Due to one person who I reported to, my work environment was toxic and stressful. Furthermore, I didn't like the culture in Florida whether it was at work or home. I started becoming depressed and spent every morning in the parking lot of my employer crying and praying for a way to change my circumstances. God gives us free will to make choices based on what we believe is best for us. I have always made choices with the best intentions, but unfortunately at times, without the best information.

One morning, I was so emotionally drained that I took the day off. I sat in silence and concluded that I would have to resign immediately. I reminisced about that moment in the past when I realized you can't have faith and fear. I decided to take a leap of faith, called my cousin Nancy and explained everything that I had been going through over the past seven months. Her answer was, *"pack your bags, you can come live here for as long as you need."* I felt my spirit lift and my prayers answered. *"If Allah intends good for someone, then he afflicts him with trials."* (Sahih Al-Bukhari)[2]

Allah only wants the best for us. So, instead of seeing tests as a punishment, we should treat them as an opportunity to express gratitude, exercise patience and remind ourselves of Allah's power and authority. When learning how to deal with life's adversities through Islamic values, look no further than the Prophet Jesus (as), Prophet Ayyub (as) and Prophet Muhammad (as) and many more. These prophets were given various challenges throughout their life and despite the misfortunes, they handled them with perseverance, integrity, and a strong belief

---

[2]   http://islam.ru/en/content/story/patience-trials-and-tribulations

in Allah. When faced with a plague that killed tens of thousands of Muslims, the companions of Prophet Muhammad remained optimistic, patient and reflective.

Perseverance

Once I was safely in Maryland and had the space to reflect on my time in Florida, I realized God gave me exactly what I asked for and what I had been through was a blessing. Although it may have been an arduous experience, I asked God to give me a job opportunity back east at a community college and not only did I get that, but it was the largest and one of the most well-known community colleges in the country. Did God want me to suffer? Of course not! God wants us to have faith, patience, and gratitude, and he will always test us because to whom much is given much is required. All that God wanted me to do was to trust Him and ask not that he get me out of my dilemma but let Him in and walk with me. God doesn't stop every negative situation instead He uses adversity to move us to our destiny. I ended up landing a VP position within two months and subsequently bought a townhouse one month later. Great tests bring on great testament, patience is one of the greatest tests one can ever face. Our prophets faced them continually.

The story of Prophet Ayub's resilience, perseverance, and patience in dealing with Allah's tribulations is one of the many stories recorded in the Qur'an. He was a righteous servant and respected man, who had been blessed with countless rewards and wealth, but then was afflicted by great suffering and illness for a long period and lost his family except for his wife. His illness was so severe that not a single limb was free from the disease, except for his tongue and heart, which he used to constantly remember Allah. Not only did he not complain or reject his fate, but Prophet Ayub would also praise and glorify God, supplicating and making dua (prayer) constantly, with whatever was left of his strength. One day, his wife asked why he didn't supplicate to relieve his illness. The reply of the prophet was, "I lived seventy years in prosperity and health, why shouldn't I be patient for the sake of Allah for seventy years." After turning to Allah and calling fervently upon Him, his call was answered. As a result of his perseverance and resilience, the prophet was once again blessed with sustenance from Allah. Together with his health, his wealth and children were restored, and he was granted even more.

When we are preoccupied with worldly life and surrounded by good things, we are likely to give less time and attention to our spiritual life. In the face of trials and tribulations, we should try our utmost to endure and persevere. These two are great habits which we can try to inculcate every day. There's nothing that patience falls upon that isn't difficult, so trust in Allah that he has the best plans for you. Muslims will be tested, especially in these times. May Allah always grant patience and *sabr* (perseverance).

CHAPTER THREE

O people, we created you all from male and female
And made you into different communities and different tribes
So that you should come to know one another
Acknowledging that the most noble among you
Is the one aware of God
Qur'an 49:13

Spiritual Transformation

When I began posting messages from a dua (prayer) or something about Ramadan on Facebook, people would say *"when did you become Muslim?"* The reaction in my head was, *"why did you assume otherwise?"* It's not surprising that sometimes people that you love and/or have spent time with are unaware of your most intimate thoughts and desires. There are certain things like religion, sex, and identity that I have always kept to myself, particularly around my deepest thoughts because of fear of judgement, criticism or just being deemed as part of the out-group. I have loved education and learning my whole life, but most people didn't know this about me, so when I completed my doctorate, folks were utterly shocked. I got the same reaction around Ramadan. Most of my life, I never claimed a religion. I just always stated my belief in and love of God.

For me, Ramadan was filled with many dichotomies, yet as I learned more about Islam, I understood ways to connect my thoughts and perceptions. I had celebrated Ramadan several times over 20 years, but Ramadan 2020 was spiritually one of the most inspirational, profound, and enlightening. I began searching for ways to connect to the outside world spiritually because, like many, COVID had me somewhat depressed. Ramadan was so impactful that I was encouraged to create videos on Facebook to share of my journey from start to finish. During the epidemic, videos were a critical method of inspiring people to become more aware of their lives…and to my surprise… awaken an interest in Ramadan. Ramadan was my saving grace. I spent a significant amount of time learning and teaching.

In this lifetime, we will certainly go through trials and hardship, and subsequently we need to seek guidance from Allah with patience. We must not forget all our blessings and the rewards that we should be thankful for. The favor and mercy of God are the only things that we need in our daily lives to overcome challenges while being grateful that we are blessed with so much. So, I learned to always trust in Allah's plan and never forget to express my gratitude to Him. Alhamdulillah.

Seeking Knowledge

The first revelation that Allah revealed to Prophet Muhammad (pbuh) was the commandment for his people to seek knowledge through the spirit of *"Iqra"*. Iqra is a command to read the signs that God has placed in the world so that all of us can understand His mercy and wisdom. It is a command to learn, through understanding and experience. And as humans continue seeking knowledge, always remember never to be arrogant knowing what we have acquired. This resonated with me significantly since I am a learner. I began reading the Qur'an daily along with many other teachings of Islam. The combination of learning about Islam and celebrating Ramadan allowed me to share my experience in a more meaningful and genuine manner.

I came across a great story about the value of knowledge. A giant ship engine failed. The ship's owner tried one expert after another, but none of them could figure out how to fix it. They eventually found an old man who had been fixing ships since he was a young man. He carried a large bag of tools with him, and when he arrived, he immediately went to work. He inspected the engine thoroughly from top to bottom. Two of the ship's owners watched the man hoping that he knew what to do. After examining things, the old man pulled a small hammer out of his bag and began gently tapping something. Suddenly, the engine sprang into life, it was fixed. He carefully put his hammer away and left. A couple of days later, the owners received a bill from the old man for $10,000 dollars. They were appalled "What he hardly did anything!" they exclaimed. They wrote the man and asked, "Please send an itemized bill." The man sent a bill that read:

Tapping with a hammer: $2.00
Knowing where to tap: $9,998[3]

The moral of the story is, you can have all the right tools but without the knowledge of how to use them, your effort is futile. Allah encourages us to gain knowledge through prayer and spiritual reading so that we are equipped to use tools like intuition, intellect, awareness, emotions, kindness, discernment, love, etc. in meaningful ways.

Ramadan Knowledge

I remember how awesome I felt with beginning to fast. I didn't feel hungry, lightheaded, or tempted to eat or drink.

---

[3]   Author unknown

For the first time, it felt like I was beginning an out-of-body experience. The calling I received to fast was so spiritual…as was everything else that was happening to me during that time. I kept noticing a strong gravitational pull towards everything that I had interest in. I was encouraged to share my experience. I remember how much I was enjoying Ramadan, how special it was making me feel, and unbeknownst to me how it was changing my life. There was an overwhelming feeling of appreciation for the things that I had in my life, both big and small. I did a lot of reflecting and asked Allah to teach me patience. I did not know that soon, I was about to be taught patience in one of the most profound ways.

It was shared with me that the last ten days of Ramadan were very special. I was told that if I stayed deeply in prayer and asked for what I wanted most and needed, they would be answered, and sins of the past would be forgiven. Also, the last ten days of Ramadan were an opportunity to gain many rewards by giving sadaqa (charity) to those in need for the sake of seeking the pleasure of Allah. So, during the last ten days of Ramadan 2020, I prayed for Allah to teach me patience, unbeknownst to me, that ask would take me on a spiritual journey that would leave me puzzled and, in more heartache, than I have ever experienced in my lifetime. The Qur'an tells us that true patience comes when heartbreak has struck us yet whoever is patient and endures, Allah will forgive them of their sins. As I mentioned before, if Allah wants to do good to someone, he afflicts them with challenges. The Prophet (pbuh) said, *"The real patience is at the first stroke of a calamity."* (Hadith number 372, narrated by Anas bin Malik from Sahih Bukhari). I had no idea that in May 2021, I would experience a misfortune. It was my time reading the Qur'an that gave me inner peace and substantial appreciation for the Prophet Muhammed. I created video vignettes of my journey through Ramadan and shared them on Facebook. Here is a description of each experience.

Video - Day one:104 view

I began my conversation about the sacrifice you make when fasting, and that it was amazing but hard. I talked about how fasting brings you on par with people that don't have a meal or drinking water. I discussed that when it was time to break the fast, the first thing I did was grab water. It felt so good, I was so thirsty, but immediately something happened. I got very emotional and explained that after drinking the water, I began crying because I realized that I had so much abundance and there were so many that didn't have water, especially children. So, I know fasting is working because I felt exactly what God wanted me to feel. I said in the video, I pray for you, I pray you stay healthy, that God provides you with abundance, covers you, and guides and protects you. I stated that, I fast every day to give back to the world what I've been blessed with, abundance, by my father, God, Allah. As salaam alaikum.

Video - Week one: 130 Views

In this video I shared I had just finished my first week of Ramadan and it had been amazing. One thing that had resonated the most had been gratitude. I had been grateful for every meal, every sip of water, for waking up another day and the opportunity to make change and be different and bring something different to the world. Grateful for the abundance that I had and that I can help others. Grateful that I could still call my mom and my family because they hadn't been affected by COVID-19. Grateful for my friends, my dog, and my neighbors. Grateful that I had a home and a job and not home-less and jobless like so many. I said that I still cried every time I broke fast because I knew that not everyone could eat or drink. I was grateful to be a child of God because I know that Allah blessed me even when I made mistakes. So, I stated saying that I pray for everyone every day by name or just association and I hope they showed gratitude for the things that they have.

Video – Day 20: 129 View

I spoke about how amazing Ramadan had been. I spoke of associating weight loss with carrying pain and that once I made the correlation, the weight was easy to remove. I reflected on how through Ramadan I could release the pain spiritually and along with it went the weight. I invited everyone to clean out their emotional, spiritual, and physical closet. I stated that anything worth going through is going to have some difficulty, pain, and confusion but it's meaningful in the end.

Video - Last day: 300 Views

Spoke of the great feeling of just completing Fajr and know-ing that I wanted to continue praying like I had been for Ramadan. I stated feeling a little sad that Ramadan was end-ing because of how much I enjoyed the journey. I learned a lot about forgiving yet needing to pay more attention to detail. I spoke of paying attention to detail and unfortunately, I still didn't learn this lesson well in 2021. I spoke of charity and doing an act of kindness because it was the right thing to do for another human being. The lessons were hard but fruitful. I encouraged everyone to pray and go after the things that make them better.

Video - Summary: 123 Views

I spoke about sacrifice, discipline, and surrender. I spoke about being one with those that don't have, being charitable, and praying for everyone and a better world. I discussed being disciplined and praying every day, five times a day, shedding tears of joy and pain. I shared how I had to learn again about letting go and surrendering. I spoke about the vulnerability of being vulnerable and how it allows you to be open to trust and love even when you're receiving dishonesty and faulty love. I reflected on how I tried to control things instead of letting God do the work. I missed the warning signs and said that it wouldn't happen again (it did though). I spoke about losing 20 pounds of baggage and realizing that those pounds were associated with pain and that I planned to keep cleaning my emotional, physical, and spiritual closet. In conclusion, I stated that in my last 10 days of Ramadan instead of just asking for what I wanted most, I claimed it. I shared understanding that preparation is key for following your purpose. Knowing that Allah is going to provide and all you have to do is follow the path of faith.

For Muslims, Ramadan is a time for spiritual reflection and growth, to help those in need, and to spend time with loved ones. Throughout Ramadan, I spent time everyday learning duas in Arabic, learning about the Prophet by reading Hadiths, and ingesting knowledge from other Muslims. Islam asks us to have knowledge, to be learners, because to have knowledge of Allah it is necessary to have knowledge of ourselves. The scholar Imam Al-Ghazali states that *"the two essential qualities of a Muslim's character are patience and gratitude. And all that patience is, is gratitude at the times of hardship. And gratitude is patience at the time of ease."* Throughout my story, I had faced many situations where patience and gratitude were the ingredients that nurtured my soul and guided my steps. I often wondered, how could I appreciate the pain I'm going through, how do I say and mean Alhamdulillah when I cannot stop the tears from falling, or the feeling of inadequacy. I can tell you from experience that saying *"alhamdulillah ala kulli haal (all praise to Allah upon all conditions)"* when you are going through your worst, is one the greatest prayers for patience and gratitude. It's common not to realize our blessings when we are navigating through the weeds but praising Allah will guide you to your highest high during your lowest lows.

Here's the crazy thing about Ramadan 2020, I learned some amazing lessons and then by Ramadan 2021, I stopped being discerning. I believe that this is when Allah began testing me again, began putting obstacles in my path, began checking my faith and obedience. There is a saying *"an obstacle is something you see when you take your eyes off of your goal"*, I forgot that our goal should be to please Allah and listen to his voice and words. I forgot that love doesn't intentionally hurt, and most importantly, you cannot fix a person who is broken, that is only something Allah can do. Allah had to test my ability to listen, it was painful, but I am stronger, wiser, and blessed beyond words. Mashallah.

*The Qur'an says, no soul can carry the burden of
another soul. I'm with you as long as you establish
prayer. Remember me and I will remember you.*

CHAPTER FOUR

Ayatul Kursi

*Allah – there is no deity except Him, the Ever-Living, the
Sustainer of [all] existence.
Neither drowsiness overtakes Him nor sleep.
To Him belongs whatever is in the heavens and
whatever is on the earth.
Who is it that can intercede with Him except by His permission?
He knows what is [presently] before them and what will be
after them, and they encompass not a thing of
His knowledge except for what He wills.
His Kursi extends over the heavens and the earth,
and their preservation tires Him not.
And He is the Most High, the Most Great.*
The Holy Qur'an Al-Baqara 2:255

Shahada

Spiritual alignment is critically meaningful. Cars run properly when aligned, the spine needs to be aligned for the body to be properly balanced, and the same is true for the spirit. Our body, mind, and spirit must all be facing the same path to move forward. Many people will go through life not realizing that they are spiritually out of alignment. However, those who have experienced it know what it's like to need an adjustment, need purpose, crave stability. I was very aware after Ramadan that I needed alignment…with a bulldozer!

Before deciding to take Shahad, the Muslim declaration of belief in the oneness of Allah and the acceptance of Muhammed as God's prophet, I did a lot of soul searching. I reached out to many organizations and two people that I trusted for advice, my mom and Aatif. My mother told me that as long as I kept God first, she completely respected my choice in how I did it. Once again, my mother supported me during an important transition. My brother Aatif told me that he would be there all the way to guide me, pray with me, and teach my all the lessons he learned about being Muslim however he made it clear that my journey with Allah would be mine alone. Initially, I was concerned with the dichotomy of being viewed as a good Muslim and openly Gay. The book *Homosexuality in Islam* states that in the Qur'an 49:13, *it is implied that no Muslim is better than another because of any social categories that we used to classify ourselves, such as race, ethnicity, economic class, gender, or sexual orientation.* It goes on to state that, *many Muslims hold on to suppositions when it comes to issues of gender and sexuality and feel that they already know "what Islam says" without reflecting on whether they have based their belief on patriarchal culture or knowledge of religion.* I never felt that Allah loved me less for my lifestyle, and as a result, I wanted to explore the next phase of my life living for Him and gaining knowledge of the truth.

One day I found out about a wonderful Imam, Daayiee Abdullah. I didn't know at the time that he was one of only a handful of openly gay Imam's in the world. He was a scholar, entrepreneur, lawyer, and author. I reached out to him, and he graciously accepted my invitation for a discussion. He told me that when I was ready, if I became ready, he would conduct my

Shahada. I remember feeling very excited and at the same time apprehensive because everyone that I loved stated that my life would change forever. In the book, *Conversations with God*, God speaks through the author and says that *"It is doubt about ultimate outcome that has created your greatest enemy, which is fear."* I had to remind myself that you cannot have faith and fear, so I allowed my soul to carry me through and decided to take the Shahada. Because of COVID, my Shahada was virtual, and it included my Imam and two witnesses, one of which was my brother Aatif. It was a beautiful ceremony and although there were no hugs, celebratory meal, and I was alone after it ended, I felt a sense of peace, belonging and love. I have been experiencing that enlightenment since day one of Shahadah. Let me share what I've experienced about love and success since taking Shahadah, it begins with forgiveness, faith, and vulnerability.

Forgiveness

Forgiveness is one of the most painful acts of trust and humility that you will ever face. It implores you to let go of the pain inside that prevents you from experiencing your true joy. It makes you must trust in God that He will handle the person, place or thing that caused you anguish. You are encouraged internally, spiritually, with meeting that situation that hurt you and embracing it with love, not hate. It is one of the nearest acts of being with Allah and His angels that you will ever encounter. You will be faced with seeing the beauty in your pain. Even in writing this I am shedding tears of sorrow…for you and me. Let your tears free you and become raindrops that wash your path clean of fear, guilt, remorse, anger, resentment, and judgement. Let me share a piece of my journey.

Within a two-week span, I went from having a family, a community, a three-bedroom townhouse, to no family, no community, and living alone in a one-bedroom apartment with only my voice and prayers. My friends looked at me with pity, I was ashamed of myself and yet my heart was filled with forgiveness and empathy. When my partner and I separated…it was one of the hardest things that I ever experienced because I didn't see it coming…but I felt compelled to forgive because I knew the only other recourse would have been anger, resentment, and revenge. It made no sense for me to display feelings of hate towards someone that I had deeply loved and loved without fear. I allowed myself to be vulnerable for the first time in my life, I put everything on the line and wasn't afraid of losing, that was my choice, how do you blame someone for *your* choice? In all honesty, I should have used discernment and adhered to the many red flags but I believe Allah wanted me to love with reckless abandon. If I had loved with fear, I would have proceeded with uncertainty instead of assurance, imperfection instead of acceptance, and emotional absence instead of present abundance. Although forgiving and fearless, I was hurt, brokenhearted and betrayed thoughtlessly. Allah knew all along what this path would lead to and expected me to be forgiving and stand in faith…it was all I could do, only He had control. Probably one of the hardest attributes to grasp when dealing with loss is observing patience or Sabr. Allow yourself time to heal, and not let it take a toll on you. This was hard for me because I was in an unknown territory. Sabr enables a Muslim to demonstrate reliance and contentment to the decree of Allah. This will also allow that person to be grateful to Allah despite such loss knowing that Allah will never burden a soul with more than he/she can bear and that He designed that crucial moment to pay off the loss with something much bigger in the future. The Prophet Muhammad (pbuh) reminds us that a true believer will express gratitude to Allah, if prosperity attends that person, and he/she will patiently endure any adversity that befalls her, thinking that it is for her best interests. Although I realized I had to rely on God to get me through the heartbreak, another chapter was unfolding simultaneously.

I was inspired to build a legacy for my family and give sadaqah and zakat (charity), so I began a small business in real estate. My first venture started with a huge learning curve, but I was determined to be diligent and make it work. I wanted to start something scintillating and remarkable, something that would make my loved ones proud. Things began rocky and bumpy, but I was excited and figured Allah would help smooth out the rough edges. I didn't realize that Allah was about to test me again. At a certain point, I had to acquire more funding and one of my friends introduced me to private lenders. They came onboard with enthusiasm but that steadily turned into badgering. It changed into constant threats about things that were out of my control, but I feared not because I knew Allah would cover me. I was facing daunting stress and feeling immensely alone. I tried to make the petty ills of these people not disturb my equanimity, but it affected me greatly. So, I did the only thing that I could, I prayed and stayed in faith. I recall speaking to one of those lenders and asked her if we could remain Godlike in our interactions, since they were *Christians*, her answer changed everything, and I knew I would prevail. She said, "*God has nothing to do it*". In the end, I worked with someone who obtained a lawyer and we were able to get rid of them. Even though I basically lost all my money and was stressed beyond words, I gained confidence and strength in myself. In addition, I knew Allah had greater things planned for me and it was only a matter of time before the light would shine a lot brighter.

Upon reflection, I began to see why my Muslim family said that when I take Shahadah my life would change forever.

It did, the tests were greater, the losses were harder, and the lessons were enormous. One of many important things that I have learned is that the greatest asset you have with taking on challenges is finding that sweet spot in your heart so that your spirit isn't compromised. If you're struggling with affliction or loss, turn to God, if your relationship is on the rocks, surrender, not necessarily to fix those challenges but to bring you a sense of balance and peace. When you feel you have lost everything, that is the time to go into intense introspection, not about what you have lost but about what you will find. Holding onto faith is very hard, believe in the unseen and praise Allah for the good AND the bad of what you are experiencing.

Faith

The dictionary defines *faith* as "belief in, devotion to, or trust in somebody or something, especially without logical proof."[4] It also defines *faith* as "belief in and devotion to God. According to the Bible, faith is belief in the one, true God without actually seeing Him.[5] In Islam, it is recognized that faith is affirmation and not merely belief. Affirmation includes the words of the heart, which is belief, and the actions of the heart, which is compliance. Hence, faith in Islam means to believe in Allah, to affirm His truth, and to submit to His commands.

Throughout my life, I have been told that I must have faith when facing adversity. I didn't truly understand what that meant until I was tested, until I was at what I believed to be my worst. I have come to the notion that your worst is subjective to the time that you are going through it. My faith in Allah,

---

4   https://www.merriam-webster.com/dictionary/faith
5   https://www.gotquestions.org/Bible-faith.html

and subsequently myself, has been tested time and time again. I felt like I was going through a similar story to the Prophet Job, staying steadfast in faith while watching everything around me crumble. Life is full of trials and tribulations, and nobody is free from hardship. Even the prophets and messengers were tested with challenges such as loss of wealth, health and loved ones. Have you been faced with a situation that you see no way of getting out of? Do you look at the issues that society is facing today and wonder how they can ever be solved? The timeless story of Prophet Yunus teaches us that there is always a way out if only we have faith.

Prophet Yunus was sent to preach to the people of Nineveh, a great city that had become filled with wickedness. But the people of his city rejected him, just as many nations rejected the messengers before him. When he realized he did not achieve what he had hoped for and failed this mission, he left disheartened. Having left the city without the permission of Allah, he boarded a ship to set sail far away from the city. Once at sea, a massive storm grew stronger and stronger, and the ship sank. After drawing lots (making a chance decision by using straws or pebbles) three times, Yunus was the one to leave the ship.

In the water, something extraordinary happens. As Allah commanded, a whale was sent to swallow Yunus whole, and then descended to the bottom of the sea. Faced with total despair, engulfed by darkness and to the deep sea, it was in the depths of despair that things changed for him. Even though he was a religious man and called upon to be a prophet, he sought help from Allah, as it is only Allah and not him, who was in control of all things. The whale swam to the surface and ejected Yunus onto the shore. Then with the help of Allah, a plant grew over him to cover the prophet with its shade. And after his recovery from the ordeal, he sets to return to Nineveh to discover then that the city and its people had not been destroyed by the terrible storm, as they have all turned to Allah.[6]

If you ever felt like you are in the belly of a whale surrounded by darkness, despair and seemingly no way out, do what the Prophet did, stay indefatigable, and have faith and trust in God. This is critical now as we face incredible circumstances like pandemics, antiracism, and climate crisis. These present times may be difficult and certainly alarming to many people but one thing's for sure - as Muslims, turning to our faith during this period is the first step to navigating the new truths of life. For the hardships are those blessed opportunities for us to raise our faith towards Allah.

I wanted to invite you to another way of looking at faith. Allah doesn't orchestra our tragedies. Did you ever consider that EVERY time you walk, drive or are driven, meet a new person, work, stand in place, breathe air, fly, take the train, etc., that you probably missed something going wrong by seconds, minutes, or hours because of Allah? Allah loves us but doesn't always prevent us from danger. I had a friend that was diagnosed with COVID on a Friday, was in the hospital on the following Monday, and subsequently died on Sunday, nine days later. Never forget that we have free will of where we go, who we are around, yet tragedy can exist within the best intentions. Wickedness or tragedy finds its way into our lives sometimes because of our choices but it doesn't mean, our choices were bad or good, it is just a part of our path. For example, my friends have disdain for my former partner because of what she put me through but at the end of the day, it was my choice to trust her and ignore the warning signs. If you stay in faith, the obstacles formed on your paths become easier to bear. By knowing that Allah doesn't make mistakes no

---

[6]   https://www.havehalalwilltravel.com/prophet-stories-islam-quran

matter how bad the circumstance, you will find peace and balance. Allah told Moses *"O Moses! Do not be afraid! Messengers should have no fear in My presence. Fear is only for those who do wrong."* Always give thanks when you wake up knowing that each step you take, the air you breathe, the choice you make, is divinely prepared. Live your life without fear, you cannot practice faith while entertaining fear.

Vulnerability

It is amazing how many people view vulnerability as a weakness when it is the best demonstration of strength. Dr. Brené Brown defines vulnerability as uncertainty, risk, and emotional exposure. I always felt that being vulnerable was always the ultimate way of knowing that I had met my soulmate because I could love unconditionally. I always wanted to experience that deep feeling of love, trust, honesty, and kindness with someone. Previously I allowed myself to fall deeply in love and although I made the wrong choice in the person, I still believe there's truth to my notion. I was fearless. If you reflect on some of the most dramatic moments in your life, you'll see that the times when you felt most vulnerable were the times when you should have the most courage. When you lay it all on the line, many times it is not done correctly, not done thinking clearly, not reading the red flags, it's just done from the heart. The test is how we handle the disappointment that comes with the pain we expose ourselves to. When we stand up to shame, fear, humility and admit that we made a mistake without judgement we reap the benefits and learning of embracing vulnerability. Embracing shame and humility allows us to experience empathy, gratitude, accountability, self-awareness, and personal growth.

Vulnerability allows us to have the courage to put prophetic goodness into action for the sake of all of those whose peace is being disrupted. The most important lesson that I learned is that we will never be able to be as vulnerable with a human being as we are with Allah. Allah will never hurt us. Vulnerability is difficult. It requires a great deal of humility and trust especially when we face challenges that are more personal than we are comfortable sharing. Weaknesses can be hard to admit, and I think this is especially true when it comes to talking with God. The times when I have approached God with vulnerability were those times when I was the most broken. That is not to say my prayers were not always sincere, but there is a stronger, more heartfelt longing for God and His Word when I have reached breaking points in my life.

Every time I have asked Allah to point out the places in my life that need the most work, I feel a sense of anxiety about what He might reveal to me. I don't think any of us like working through our hardships and raw emotions but imagine what our lives would be like when we intentionally do it, anyway.

CHAPTER FIVE

O Allah, whatever blessing has been received
by me in the morning (evening)
or anyone of Your creation is from You alone,
You have no partner.
All praise is for you and thanks is to You.
Abu Dawud 4/318, Ibn As-Sunni (Hadith no.
41), Ibn Hibban (Hadith no. 2361)

Harmony

The Merriam Webster definition of harmony is an "interweaving of different accounts into a single narrative and the definition of soul is a person's deeply felt moral and emotional nature." Hence the harmony of my soul is the "beautiful arrangements of the parts of my spirituality." Living in harmony is like living in balance, you have to find the perfect mix of gratitude, contentment, tranquility and among the many aspects life encompasses. However, a harmonious life is also contingent on the people and circumstances around you. Building harmony means accepting everything you are, have been and will become. I realize that the greatest reminder of love, kindness, and joy is the voice within. Your thoughts and actions begin and end with the voice that is capturing and relaying your soul's ultimate desire, to create a better you.

Although I have faced adversity many times in my life, I have to say I have never experienced them happening one after another, and all very painful. The plethora of misfortune was not familiar to me, and most times was extremely uncomfortable. I know that my choice to embrace and accept Islam when I did was no coincidence, I needed it. As I mentioned, I was going through several difficult situations happening at once, a sudden and thoughtless breakup, a business investment that would go awry at the eleventh hour and losing almost all the money from the sale of my house. Moments were spent crying in the shower, doubled over in agony, asking Allah to help me sleep, eat, and find the strength to cope, while managing a demanding job. The answer that would come to me often was *"you are stronger than you think, be patient, for I am holding you."* I listened intently and with time I began learning, learning how to surrender to compassion and patience in ways that I never would have had I not been praying five or more) times a day. They were not easy lessons; I didn't enjoy any aspect of it or feel stable. At one point I was experiencing anguish and pain all day, from morning until night…it was depression. Over time, the pain changed and would visit mainly in the morning or evening. I let work consume my every thought and feeling throughout the afternoons, literally. Although I felt everything…I felt nothing. My brother Aatif was my lifeline. He called me every day, sometimes twice a day, to remind me that what I was going through was by design. I was right where I was supposed to be, and Allah was well aware. I began to accept that although I had free will, Allah wanted me to go through those excruciating experiences, to be prepared for a felicitous and prosperous journey. So how does one's soul find harmony? Spirit began sending me messages in the weirdest and sometimes most awkward places.

Seeds of Life

One day I was preparing to plant flowers in my former home. I began digging up the soil only to find heavy rock and clay deep beneath the surface. I realized in that moment that it was necessary to dig up the earth at its core, its foundation… its *heart and soul*…in order for it to flourish. Those seeds cannot be expected to grow at their full potential if the soil is not adequately churned, replaced, and watered. Like our lives, we can't expect to get different results if we keep planting our seeds, our growth, in unhealthy behavior, habits, and conditions. Allah will keep giving us chances to be discerning, to grow, to make mistakes, however "to whom much is given, much is required." Our soul is ever knowing, and it is important that we nourish it with our true and authentic selves. Ask yourself, am I trying to create a healthy foundation layered with gravel and underpinnings? If so, start digging. It will be painful at first but like a beautiful flower, you will begin to bloom. In Conversations with God, the author narrates God saying *"You can know yourself to be generous, but unless you do something which displays generosity, you have nothing but a concept. You can know yourself to be kind, but unless you do someone a kindness, you have nothing but an idea about yourself."* You can know yourself to be strong, but until you do something that indicates perseverance, you have nothing but hopelessness. Being aware of myself came with letting go of judgement, control, and expectations. I know myself to be giving and loving but realized that I had to forgive to continue being my genuine self. When you break down the description of harmony, it all comes down to the parts. Take time to evaluate all your parts: your health (physical and mental), your family (including animals), your spirituality, your career, your friends, your hobbies, your dreams, your desires, etc. How much time and attention do you give to each part or require from each? Is there discord in any of the parts that prevents you from rising to a higher vibration or becoming your best self? If so, are you changing your circumstances or just settling?

Change

Change is hard. Changing the parts of your life that disrupt harmony is no small feat because it usually means the people or circumstances around you will have to change, and that can sometimes come with pain, sadness, and disappointment. When I began searching my soul for answers, I realized I wasn't asking the right questions. I first began by asking the dreaded WHY? Why is this happening to me? Why is my loved one sick? Why did I lose my home? Why did she leave me? Why am I in so much pain? Why am I not healthy? Why COVID? Why did Allah let this happen? I could go on and on. My brother helped me to see that we don't question why when everything was going well so WHY now? It caught me off guard because it was so true. I never ask why when everything was going well nor did I take it for granted, I just stay in gratitude. He told me to say, *"Alhamdulillah ala kulli haal,"* which means Praise Allah for all conditions. I began asking WHAT and HOW. What can I do to make the pain stop? How can I change my thoughts? What can I do to please Allah? How can my health get better? What can I do differently? How can I fill the hole in my heart? What is needed in my life to create harmony?

Change, although necessary, can be very daunting. With it comes uncertainty, discomfort, lack of control, and for those of us who prosper on stability, change can be challenging to accept.

But if we don't change, we miss out on some of the most amazing things in life: growth, opportunity, and evolution. So just as we accept the changing leaves as summer turns to fall, we need to embrace the transitions in our own lives. Because so many bests – best moments, best days, best versions of ourselves – are ahead, just waiting for us to achieve them.

Allah's Voice

Your journey in life began at birth, and believe it or not, so your path began. In Conversations with God, it is stated *"for most of your life you have lived at the effect of your experiences. Now, you're invited to be the cause of them. That is what is called conscious living."* When we come to a place of awareness of Self because of life experiences, we bring a new outlook on the concept of right and wrong. With awareness we then begin to appreciate and accept that there really is no such thing as right or wrong, there just is. If you can accept that your path was laid out for you at birth, and although you were given free will to make choices and others may have made choices for you, you're still on the path that Allah made for you. I read a quote that said, *"an obstacle is something you see when you take your eyes off of your goal."* This can be the same for taking your eyes off your path. Let me give a personal example. I was in a relationship that would never last, and although I was receiving warning signs to use discernment, my heart was guiding my better reasoning. Allah already knew the choices that I was going to make, the path was established. It was up to me if I was going to make it easy and walk away with my heart in tack, or difficult with my heart broken. I chose the latter and paid dearly, I just wasn't listening to Him. Allah speaks to us through songs, through our friends, through seeing how one treats others, through books, and the best one, the most important way, is through what people tell us about themselves. You have to listen!

Allah is all merciful, and He made us able to express ourselves through speech and thought. He provides us with everything we need and loves us immensely. He does not speak to us directly, but He makes us feel Him. If we speak or pray to Him, He will always hear us and see us, and He will respond to our prayers as He wishes. Remember, if God deprives us and we lose our loved ones, health, job, wealth, or family, but at the same time, He opens the doors of understanding, then this is not deprivation. It is in fact a gift; we are moving closer to Him through patience and faith.

The Soul's Purpose

The first step to uncovering and aligning with your soul's purpose is to take away anything that is not in your highest good. Please note that I stated, "take away" and not "move away from." When you *take away* you are consciously removing or eliminating it from your space, your thoughts, and your being. It is gone. On the other hand, when you *move away from* something, it isn't gone and you're allowing room to come back to it. This is extremely important because your soul encompasses your spirit, consciousness, and self and to strive towards your highest vibration, it is imperative that you clear space for Allah to join you. How can your deeply felt moral and emotional self find its purpose if you are not at peace? How can Allah help you if you do not take away anything that keeps you from your authentic self? All He wants is for us to be our best.

One of the pillars of Islam is that Muslims pray five times a day. Before those prayers, we are expected to perform a purification ritual called *wudu*, requiring that we wash our face, hands, arms, and feet. We pray directly to Allah and believe that, out of humility and respect for the Almighty, one should prepare to do so with a clean heart, mind, and body. This ritual of cleansing is symbolic of how we reach our soul's purpose. We remove difficulties, pain, uncertainty, and scarcity and replace it with tranquility, joy, confidence, and abundance. That can only be achieved by "taking away" anything that does not serve a higher purpose in your life.

CONCLUSION

Serenity Prayer

God, grant me
Serenity to accept the things
I cannot change
Courage to change,
the things I can
and
Wisdom to
know the difference.

How can you create harmony in your soul? How can you eradicate barriers that prevent you from the blessings Allah has for you? What would you do differently *if you knew* what Allah had planned for you? How would you feel if you knew that for all the heartbreak, loss, disappointment, pain and betrayal that you experienced because of mistakes or trusting others, Allah was planning to bring you blessings unimaginable? Would you still be depressed? Would you still be consumed with anger, regret, and revenge? Would you still feel hopeless, shameful, and blame yourself? If you knew and believed that behind the scenes, Allah was working for your good, what would you do differently?

When you are searching for answers after experiencing adversity or hardship, you will receive all forms of advice. I beg you, in those times of deep sorrow, cry and release but also imagine what Allah is planning for you once you let go. Once you take away every person, place, thing, or thought that is holding you back, He will fulfill your greatest blessings. For every day that you spend in sorrow, do one small thing like, read a chapter from the Qur'an or bible, buy a journal or an uplifting book, listen to a spiritual broadcast, and talk to someone that will be patient and not judge your process. You have to trust, believe and above all have FAITH that things will get better.

In the book Emotional Detox, the author states, *when we are resistant, our energy becomes stiff, and we get stuck there. We know this because that's when we tend to overthink, causing us to protect rather than open to emotional connections, like when we treat everything as a battle and have to fight for what we need or to prove our worth.* One of the hardest things that I had to learn during my hardship, was to forgive myself, I was stuck. I beat up on myself really badly, I was ashamed, I was embarrassed, and my pride was damaged. I found myself walking with my head down, criticizing the image in the mirror, and feeling stupid for allowing myself to fall deeply in love with someone that didn't deserve me, didn't deserve my love at all. I vowed I would never allow this to happen again, ever and then I began receiving positive messages randomly.

- o *"Have patience. All things are difficult before they become easy." Saadi.*
- o *"In trusting Allah, remember that what's best for you might be what's most painful." Author unknown.*
- o *"We must be willing to let go of the life we had planned, so as to have the life that is waiting for us." Joseph Campbell.*
- o *"I'm starting over: a new pattern of thoughts, a new wave of emotions, a new connection to the world, a new belief system in myself." Author unknown.*
- o *"I thought I was broken and needed fixing. Not true! I was hurt and needed healing, A completely different concept." Author unknown.*

This message was probably the most salient of all…
- o **God is saying to you today…**
  I know every person that's done you wrong,
  every injustice, and every bad break.
  I am going to pay you back.
  You're going to come out fully compensated,
  blessed, and vindicated. Author unknown.

The process of forgiving myself started when I listened, believed, and recited these messages and remembered that I was an amazing, kind, loving, thoughtful, smart, successful attractive, spiritual and giving person, before any relationship or hardship. In addition, I learned how to listen to and see the warning signs that Allah puts before me. Allah speaks to us through our senses, our thoughts, and feelings. When you do not hear Allah, it is not because Allah is being silent, it is usually because we have stopped listening. I realized that those moments in time, regardless of how deceitful and thoughtless they played out to be, were nothing more than just a moment. I looked in the mirror and this time I could feel Allah saying let go, *take away* all that is not for your good so that I can do my work on your mind, body and soul. In those quiet moments, I could hear Allah telling me that memories of my past relationship will come and go…but He is doing things behind the scenes to show me that nothing was done by accident. I began taking away pictures, artifacts, jewelry, thoughts, discussions etc. so that I could begin receiving my blessings. My friends, the closer you are to Allah, the more you will be tested just as the Prophets were tested. Do not become despondent, sad, or depressed…this is your time. This is your time to be patient, to show gratitude, and KNOW that you will be rewarded. Allah will always give you back 10 times more than you have lost.

When you think of your life as having chapters you will realize that there are special chapters that you cannot keep reading, hoping for a different ending, you must turn the page and move on. As of writing this memoir, I am basking in happiness because although things were a little difficult financially, emotionally, and physically because of the events of the past, I am grateful because the past taught me valuable lessons, and more importantly, more than anything else brought me closer to Allah, and the harmony of my soul. Alhamdulillah.

SUGGESTED READINGS

The Qur'an. By Al-Baqara

Hadith. By Sahih Al-Bukhari

Progressive Islam – The rich liberal ideas of the Muslim faith. By Daayiee Abdullah

Conversations with God. By Neale Donald Walsch

Secrets of Divine Love – A Spiritual Journey into the Heart of Islam. By A. Helwa

Homosexuality in Islam – Critical reflection on gay, lesbian, and transgender Muslims. By Scott Siraj al-Haqq Kugle

The Spiritual Entrepreneur. By Angelina Lombardo

What Happened To You - Conversations on Trauma, Resilience, and Healing. By Bruce Perry and Oprah Winfrey

Emotional Detox – 7 Steps to Release Toxicity and Energize Joy. By Sherianna Boyle

* 9 7 9 8 2 1 8 3 1 1 4 6 9 *